Counting Money

Barbara Gannett

Sadlier-Oxford
A Division of William H. Sadlier, Inc.

Contents

Getting Started

Do you have any money? Check your pockets. Shake your piggy bank. How much do you have? Let's count to find out.

Money Chart

First you need to know what coins you have. Look at the chart.

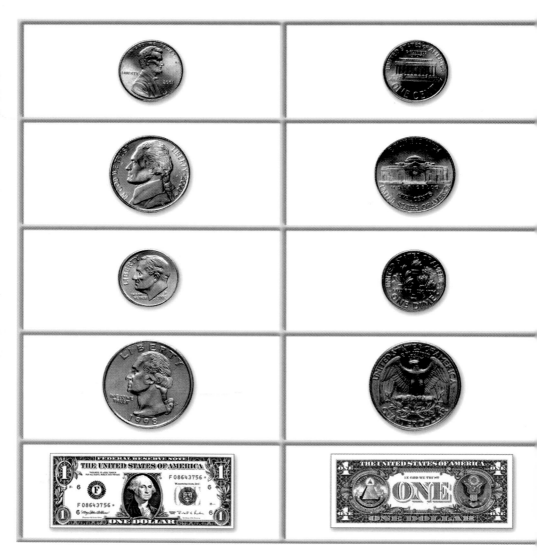

penny	1 cent or 1¢
nickel	5 cents or 5¢
dime	10 cents or 10¢
quarter	25 cents or 25¢
one dollar bill	100 cents or 100¢ 1 dollar or $1

When Coins Are the Same

If you just have pennies, it's easy to count your money. To find the value of a group of pennies, count by ones.

One hundred pennies equal one dollar.

To find the value of a group of nickels, count by fives.

Twenty nickels equal one dollar.

To find the value of a group of dimes, count by tens.

Ten dimes equal one dollar.

To find the value of a group of quarters, count by twenty-fives.

It's hard to count by twenty-fives! This chart can help.

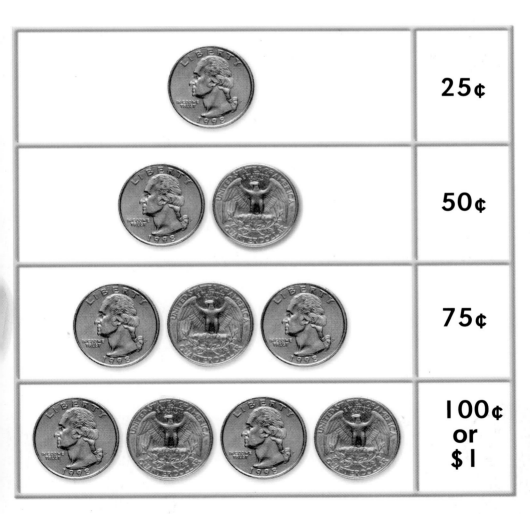

	25¢
	50¢
	75¢
	100¢ or $1

When Coins Are Different

What if you have lots of different coins? How can you count your money then?

First sort the coins. It helps to put them in rows. Start with quarters.

Then make a row of dimes.
Line up the nickels next.
Put the pennies last.

Find the value of the quarters first. When you count a coin, move it a little. That way, you won't count the same coin twice.

Two quarters equal 50¢.

When you have counted the quarters, count on by tens for each dime you have. Next count on by fives for each nickel. Then count on by ones for each penny.

Did you count 99¢?

Now you know how to count your money. Check your pockets. Empty your piggy bank. How much money do you have?

Glossary

cent sign ¢

---

dime 10¢ or

---

dollar sign $

---

nickel 5¢ or

---

one dollar bill 100¢ or $1

---

penny 1¢ or

---

quarter 25¢ or

---

value the amount of money a coin or bill is worth

My Math Project

Play Store

What You Need:

sticky notes   crayons   play coins   drawing paper

What You Do:

1. Find two things to buy in your classroom.

2. Use sticky notes to make price tags. Each thing should cost less than one dollar.

3. Find a partner. Take turns pretending to buy things from each other. Count the coins to pay.

4. Draw a picture to show something you bought. Write the price, too.

59¢

Index